The Ultimate
Employee Training
Guide
Training Today, Leading Tomorrow

Gerard Assey

Table of Contents

Preface

In a world that evolves at an unprecedented pace, the success of any organization hinges upon its ability to adapt and thrive in the face of change. The key to this adaptation, the secret ingredient that empowers businesses to not only survive but to flourish, lies within its workforce. Your employees are your most valuable assets, and their growth and development are essential for your organization's continued success.

Welcome to '**The Ultimate Employee Training Guide: *Training Today, Leading Tomorrow'*** This comprehensive guide is designed to be your compass in the ever-changing landscape of employee training. Whether you are a seasoned HR professional, a corporate leader, or someone embarking on their journey in the realm of training and development, this book is your toolkit for creating a workforce that's ready for the challenges of today and tomorrow.

A Journey of Learning and Growth

Throughout these pages, we will embark on a journey that explores the importance of training, its profound benefits, and the repercussions that stem from neglecting it. We'll delve into the concept of training as an investment, deciphering the intricate language of Return on Investment (ROI), and drawing inspiration from real-life case studies that showcase the tangible impact of effective training initiatives.

Understanding the core of your workforce's needs is paramount, and we will guide you through the process of assessing and addressing these needs comprehensively. From product knowledge gaps to skills assessments, behavior, and attitude adjustments, you'll gain insights into the tools and methods that facilitate a profound understanding of what training is truly required.

But selecting the right training is only half the battle. In this book, we'll equip you with the knowledge to choose the right training vendor, assess their reputation, customization capabilities, and balance cost versus quality considerations. You'll be armed with the tools to make informed decisions that align with your organization's unique goals and culture.

Planning and implementing training programs, the heart of any training initiative, are detailed in these chapters. You'll learn to craft a robust training strategy, design effective modules, and adapt your delivery methods to fit the needs of your audience. Monitoring and evaluation strategies will ensure that your training efforts are constantly refined and improved, resulting in an agile and adaptable training program.

As we look ahead, we delve into the future of training, exploring the technological advancements and trends that will shape the landscape of employee development. From technology-driven training solutions to the rise of micro-learning and gamification, we'll keep you at the forefront of innovation.

But the journey doesn't end there. We'll also explore how to create a culture of continuous learning within your organization, fostering career development, seeking employee feedback, and encouraging self-directed learning.

Measuring the impact of training, both qualitatively and quantitatively, is a crucial step in ensuring its success. In this book, you'll discover methods inspired by Kirkpatrick's Four Levels of Evaluation, learn to identify the right metrics for success, make data-driven decisions, and implement continuous improvement strategies.

Additionally, we will address the legal and ethical considerations that underpin training programs, covering compliance, diversity and inclusion, privacy, and intellectual property.

Our journey concludes with a look at successful case studies from various industries, showcasing how organizations have transformed their workforce through strategic training initiatives.

Finally, we reflect on the future of employee training, the pivotal role of HR and corporate leadership, and the ongoing journey of training in an ever-evolving world.

Your Guide to Training Excellence

As you read through these pages, we encourage you to embrace the knowledge and insights shared within. The ideas, strategies, and examples you encounter here are not mere theories but have been tried, tested, and proven in the real world.

Remember that employee training is not just an investment in your organization; it's an investment in the people who drive it forward. Your commitment to their growth is a testament to your vision for a brighter future.

We invite you to embark on this transformative journey with us, as together, we uncover the true potential of your workforce and, in doing so, unlock the future success of your organization.

Thank you for choosing '**The Ultimate Employee Training Guide:** *Training Today, Leading Tomorrow*'

We wish you every success on your path to training excellence.

The Importance of Training Employees

In the ever-evolving landscape of the corporate world, the role of employee training has transformed from a mere option to an absolute necessity. This chapter delves deep into the significance of training employees, tracing its evolution over time, elucidating the myriad benefits it brings, and highlighting the stark repercussions an organization can face when it neglects this crucial aspect of human resource development.

The Evolution of Employee Training

The concept of training employees is as old as organized work itself, but the methods and approaches have undergone a remarkable evolution. In the early industrial era, training was often informal, with apprenticeships and on-the-job learning being the norm. However, as industries advanced and diversified, so did the need for structured training programs.

Understanding the Historical Context

To truly appreciate the importance of employee training, one must understand its historical context. Consider the apprenticeship system in the 18th century, where skilled craftsmen passed down their knowledge to apprentices. This lineage of learning laid the foundation for structured training as we know it today.

Embracing Technological Advancements

As technology burgeoned, so did the complexity of job roles. This necessitated specialized training, which was made possible by innovations such as e-learning platforms, simulations, and virtual reality. Organizations that adapted to these changes thrived, while those that resisted fell behind.

Benefits of Employee Training

Effective employee training is a catalyst for organizational growth and competitiveness. It provides a slew of benefits that extend well beyond the individual employee. Here, we explore these advantages in depth.

Enhanced Employee Performance

When employees receive comprehensive training, they become better equipped to perform their roles with proficiency. For instance, a sales representative armed with product knowledge and sales techniques is more likely to close deals successfully. This, in turn, directly impacts the company's bottom line.

Increased Employee Engagement and Satisfaction

Investing in employee development demonstrates a commitment to their growth and success. This not only boosts morale but also fosters a sense of loyalty and engagement. Engaged employees are more likely to stay with the organization, reducing turnover rates.

Competitive Advantage

In today's fiercely competitive market, having a skilled workforce can be a game-changer. A company with a team of well-trained employees can respond more effectively to market changes, customer demands, and industry trends, thereby gaining a competitive edge.

Innovation and Adaptability

Innovation often stems from knowledge and creative thinking. Training can stimulate innovation by exposing employees to new ideas, technologies, and methodologies. Furthermore, a well-trained workforce is more adaptable to change, facilitating smoother transitions during organizational transformations.

Repercussions of Neglecting Training
Just as the benefits of training are far-reaching, so too are the consequences of neglecting this essential aspect of employee development.
Stagnation and Inefficiency
Failure to provide training can lead to stagnation within an organization. Employees may continue to perform tasks in outdated, inefficient ways, resulting in wasted time and resources.
High Turnover Rates
Employees who feel their growth is stifled are likely to seek opportunities elsewhere. High turnover rates can be a costly outcome of neglecting training, as recruiting and onboarding new talent is both time-consuming and expensive.
Decreased Morale and Engagement
When employees see a lack of investment in their development, morale can plummet. This discontent can spread like wildfire and negatively impact overall workplace culture and productivity.
Vulnerability to Market Shifts
In an era of rapid change, organizations that do not invest in training risk becoming obsolete. Market shifts, technological advancements, and evolving customer preferences can quickly render an untrained workforce irrelevant.

In conclusion, this chapter serves as a foundation for understanding why training employees is not just an option but a strategic imperative. By tracing the evolution of training, uncovering its myriad benefits, and highlighting the dire consequences of neglect, we lay the groundwork for the comprehensive exploration of employee training that follows in this book. Through real-world examples and actionable insights, we will equip you with the knowledge and tools needed to harness the power of employee training for the betterment of your organization.

Investing in Training: Understanding the ROI

In the corporate world, decisions are often scrutinized for their impact on the bottom line. In this chapter, we delve into the concept of training as a strategic investment, exploring how to measure and maximize the Return on Investment (ROI). Real-life case studies will illuminate the path, showing how organizations have successfully turned training expenditures into growth opportunities.

Training as an Investment

Before we dive into the numbers and metrics, it's crucial to shift our perspective: Training is an investment, not just an expense. When viewed as an investment, training programs take on a new level of strategic importance.

Aligning Training with Organizational Goals

Start by aligning training initiatives with the broader goals of the organization. For instance, if your company aims to expand its market share, invest in sales training that equips your team with the skills to drive growth.

Calculating the Full Cost of Training

To understand the true cost of training, consider not only the direct expenses like course materials and instructor fees but also the indirect costs, such as the time employees spend away from their regular duties. A comprehensive cost analysis provides a more accurate basis for ROI calculations.

Measuring Return on Investment (ROI)

Measuring the ROI of training is a multifaceted process that involves both qualitative and quantitative analysis. Here's a step-by-step guide:

- ✓ *Step 1: Define Clear Objectives*
  Start by defining clear and measurable objectives for your training program. For example, if you're conducting leadership development training, your objective might be to increase the number of employees promoted to leadership positions within a year.
- ✓ *Step 2: Collect Data*
  Gather data before and after the training program to assess its impact. This could include employee performance metrics, sales figures, customer satisfaction ratings, or any other relevant data points.
- ✓ *Step 3: Calculate ROI*
  The formula for calculating ROI is straightforward:
- ✓ ROI (%) = (Net Gain from Investment / Cost of Investment) x 100
- ✓ Net Gain from Investment is the difference between the benefits (e.g., increased sales or productivity) and the costs (including both direct and indirect expenses).
- ✓ *Step 4: Consider Intangible Benefits*
  While ROI is often associated with monetary gains, don't forget to consider intangible benefits like improved employee morale, better teamwork, or enhanced customer service. These aspects can have a significant impact on the overall success of your organization.

Real-Life Case Studies

Case studies provide a concrete understanding of how training investments can pay off. Let's examine a few real-life examples:

✓ *Case Study 1: Retail Sales Training*

A retail company invested in comprehensive sales training for its staff. After the training, the company saw a 15% increase in sales. Taking into account the cost of training, the ROI was calculated at 25%, indicating that for every dollar invested in training, the company gained $1.25 in revenue.

✓ *Case Study 2: Leadership Development*

A tech firm invested in leadership development programs for its middle managers. Over the course of a year, the company noticed a significant improvement in employee retention, reduced turnover costs, and increased innovation. The ROI, when considering both tangible and intangible benefits, was estimated at 150%.

✓ *Case Study 3: Customer Service Training*

A hospitality company invested in customer service training for its frontline staff. This investment resulted in a notable improvement in guest satisfaction scores and a 10% increase in repeat business. The calculated ROI was 40%, demonstrating the tangible impact of training on customer loyalty.

Training ROI Calculator

Here's an example of a Training ROI Calculator in a sample format. This Training ROI Calculator allows managers to input investment costs and expected benefits to estimate the return on investment for their training programs. It helps decision-makers assess the financial impact of training and make informed choices about allocating resources for future initiatives.

Training ROI Calculator
Training Program Name: [Insert Program Name]
Date of Calculation: [Insert Date]

Investment Costs:
Training Development Costs:
- ✓ Content Development: $___________
- ✓ Trainer/Facilitator Fees: $___________
- ✓ Materials and Resources: $___________

Training Delivery Costs:
- ✓ Venue Rental: $___________
- ✓ Equipment and Technology: $___________
- ✓ Travel and Accommodation: $___________

Participant Costs:
- ✓ Participant   Wages   During   Training: $___________
- ✓ Travel Expenses (if applicable): $___________

Administrative Costs:
- ✓ Training   Coordination   and   Administration: $___________
- ✓ Evaluation and Reporting: $___________

Total Investment Costs: $___________

Benefits and Returns:
Productivity Gains:
- ✓ Improved   Productivity   After   Training: $___________

Cost Savings:
- ✓ Reduction in Errors/Incidents: $___________
- ✓ Reduced Employee Turnover: $___________
- ✓ Increased Sales or Revenue: $___________

Quality Improvements:
- ✓ Improved Quality of Work: $___________

Time Savings:
- ✓ Time Savings Due to Increased Efficiency: $__________
- ✓ Total Benefits and Returns: $__________

ROI Calculation:
ROI (%) = (Total Benefits - Total Costs) / Total Costs × 100
ROI = ($__________ - $) / $ × 100
ROI = ______%

Decision and Analysis:
- ✓ Based on the calculated ROI, consider the following:
- ✓ An ROI above 100% indicates a positive return on investment.
- ✓ An ROI below 100% suggests that the training program may need further evaluation and improvement.
- ✓ Evaluate the results and consider whether the training program aligns with organizational goals and justifies the budget allocated.

In conclusion, this chapter underscores the critical perspective shift: training is an investment, not merely an expense. By defining clear objectives, measuring ROI, and considering both tangible and intangible benefits, organizations can make informed decisions about their training initiatives. Real-life case studies illustrate that when executed strategically, training investments can yield substantial returns, positioning training as a key driver of organizational success.

Key Skills, Attributes and Traits of an Effective Trainer

Being an effective trainer requires a combination of skills, traits, and attributes. Here are key attributes and traits of an effective trainer, along with examples:

1. Subject Matter Expertise:

Description: An effective trainer should have a deep understanding of the subject matter they are teaching.

Example: A software development trainer should be well-versed in programming languages, development tools, and industry best practices.

2. Communication Skills:

Description: Clear and effective communication is essential to convey information, engage learners, and address questions.

Example: A communication skills trainer should model effective communication techniques and provide constructive feedback to participants.

3. Adaptability:

Description: Effective trainers can adjust their teaching style to meet the needs of diverse learners and adapt to changing circumstances.

Example: In a virtual training environment, an adaptable trainer might incorporate interactive polls or breakout sessions to maintain engagement.

4. Patience:

Description: Patience is vital when working with learners who may struggle to grasp certain concepts or require additional support.

Example: A math tutor patiently explains complex equations until a struggling student comprehends the material.

5. Empathy:
Description: Empathetic trainers understand learners' perspectives, build rapport, and create a safe learning environment.
Example: An empathy-driven trainer acknowledges the challenges faced by new employees during onboarding and offers support.
6. Active Listening:
Description: Effective trainers listen attentively to learners' questions, concerns, and feedback.
Example: During a customer service training session, a trainer actively listens to employees' experiences with difficult customers and tailors the training accordingly.
7. Adaptation to Technology:
Description: In today's digital age, trainers should be comfortable using technology and learning management systems.
Example: A virtual trainer proficiently uses video conferencing tools, multimedia presentations, and interactive software for remote training.
8. Creativity:
Description: Creative trainers find innovative ways to deliver content, making learning engaging and memorable.
Example: A creativity-focused trainer uses storytelling, gamification, or role-playing to make training sessions dynamic and enjoyable.
9. Organizational Skills:
Description: Effective trainers manage time, materials, and resources efficiently to ensure training runs smoothly.
Example: A project management trainer organizes training materials, schedules sessions, and tracks progress using project management tools.

10. Adaptation to Feedback:

Description: Trainers should be open to feedback from learners and continuously improve their training methods.

Example: After a leadership development training, a trainer reviews participant feedback and adjusts the program to address areas of improvement.

11. Flexibility:

Description: Effective trainers can adjust the training plan on the fly to address unexpected challenges or opportunities.

Example: A leadership trainer may modify the training schedule to accommodate an impromptu discussion on a current leadership issue.

12. Confidence:

Description: Confidence in one's knowledge and presentation abilities instills trust and credibility in learners.

Example: A cyber-security trainer confidently explains complex security protocols and assures participants of the importance of their role in safeguarding data.

13. Approachability:

Description: Approachable trainers make learners feel comfortable seeking clarification or assistance.

Example: A compliance trainer encourages employees to ask questions about regulatory requirements without fear of judgment.

14. Passion for Teaching:

Description: Passionate trainers genuinely enjoy helping others learn and grow. - Example: A sustainability trainer's enthusiasm for environmental issues inspires participants to take action in their workplaces.

15. Evaluation and Assessment Skills:
Description: Effective trainers can assess the effectiveness of training through evaluations and adjust future sessions accordingly.
Example: A sales training manager uses key performance indicators (KPIs) to measure the impact of sales training and refines the program based on results.

By embodying these attributes and continually developing their skills, trainers can create meaningful learning experiences and empower individuals to achieve their goals.

Assessing Training Needs

Effective employee training begins with a clear understanding of what needs to be taught. In this chapter, we delve into the meticulous process of assessing training needs, a critical step that ensures training programs are targeted, relevant, and ultimately, successful. We will explore various facets of training needs assessment, from identifying knowledge gaps to assessing skills, behaviors, and attitudes, all while equipping you with practical tools and methods.

Identifying Product Knowledge Gaps

Product knowledge is the cornerstone of many businesses, especially those in sales and customer service. To identify gaps in product knowledge, follow these steps:

- ✓ *Step 1: Define Product Knowledge Standards*
  Begin by establishing clear standards for what employees should know about your products or services. These standards should cover essential features, benefits, pricing, and competitive differentiators.
- ✓ *Step 2: Assess Current Knowledge Levels*
  Conduct surveys or quizzes to assess the current knowledge levels of your employees. For example, a quiz might ask sales representatives to describe key product features or explain how your product addresses customer pain points.
- ✓ *Step 3: Analyze the Results*
  Analyze the results of your assessments to identify specific knowledge gaps. This can

help you tailor training content to address these gaps directly.

Skills Assessment and Gap Analysis

Skills assessment is crucial for roles that require specific competencies. Here's how to conduct a skills assessment and perform a gap analysis:

- ✓ *Step 1: Identify Required Skills*
  Start by listing the skills necessary for each role within your organization. For instance, a project manager may require skills in project planning, stakeholder management, and risk assessment.
- ✓ *Step 2: Evaluate Current Skill Levels*
  Use performance evaluations, skills tests, or employee self-assessments to gauge the current skill levels of your workforce. This can reveal disparities between required and existing skills.
- ✓ *Step 3: Gap Analysis and Training Planning*
  Perform a gap analysis by comparing required skills to existing skills. This analysis helps prioritize which skills need immediate attention and guides the development of training programs. For instance, if your analysis shows that project managers lack risk assessment skills, you can design targeted training modules to address this gap.

Behavior and Attitude Assessment

Training isn't limited to knowledge and skills; it also extends to shaping desired behaviors and attitudes within your workforce. Here's how to assess these intangible aspects:

- ✓ *Step 1: Define Desired Behaviors and Attitudes*
  Clearly articulate the behaviors and attitudes that align with your organizational values and goals. For example, you may desire a customer-centric attitude among your customer support team.
- ✓ *Step 2: Use Behavioral Metrics and Surveys*
  Develop metrics and surveys that evaluate employees' behaviors and attitudes. For instance, you can measure customer satisfaction scores, track employee punctuality, or use employee engagement surveys to assess attitude.
- ✓ *Step 3: Feedback and Observation*
  Regularly gather feedback from managers and peers to assess behaviors and attitudes. Observations and feedback can provide valuable insights into areas that require improvement.

Tools and Methods for Assessment

Effective assessment requires the right tools and methods. Here are some widely used approaches:

- ✓ *Surveys and Questionnaires*
  Design surveys and questionnaires to gather feedback from employees, managers, and customers. These can be useful for assessing knowledge, skills, attitudes, and behavior.
- ✓ *Skills Tests and Simulations*
  Implement skills tests and simulations that allow employees to demonstrate their capabilities in a controlled environment. For instance, a software company might use coding tests to assess programming skills.

✓ *Performance Reviews and 360-Degree Feedback*
  Leverage performance reviews and 360-degree feedback systems to gain insights into employees' strengths and areas for improvement. These approaches provide a holistic view of an individual's performance.

In conclusion, this chapter emphasizes the critical role of training needs assessment in designing effective training programs. By identifying product knowledge gaps, assessing skills, behaviors, and attitudes, and employing various assessment tools and methods, organizations can ensure their training initiatives are targeted and aligned with their objectives. This chapter equips you with the knowledge and practical steps to conduct a comprehensive training needs assessment, setting the stage for impactful and relevant training programs.

Sample Formats for Assessing Training Needs

1. Assessing Product Knowledge Gaps:

Format: Product Knowledge Quiz

Employee Name: [Insert Employee Name] Position: [Insert Employee Position]

Date: [Insert Date]

Instructions: Please answer the following questions to the best of your ability.

This quiz aims to assess your product knowledge.

Question 1: What are the key features of our flagship product?

Employee's Answer: [Employee's Response] Correct Answer: [Correct Response]

Question 2: How does our product address common customer pain points? Employee's Answer: [Employee's Response] Correct Answer: [Correct Response]

Question 3: Describe the pricing tiers for our product. Employee's Answer: [Employee's Response] Correct Answer: [Correct Response]

Analysis:

In this example, the employee's responses are compared against the correct answers to identify gaps in product knowledge. The areas where the employee's responses differ from the correct answers indicate the specific areas requiring training.

2. Skills Assessment and Gap Analysis:

Format: Skills Assessment Matrix

Employee Name: [Insert Employee Name] Position: [Insert Employee Position]

Skills Required for Position:
Project Planning
Stakeholder Management
Risk Assessment
Employee's Self-Assessment:
Project Planning: [Rating on a scale of 1-5]
Stakeholder Management: [Rating on a scale of 1-5]
Risk Assessment: [Rating on a scale of 1-5]
Manager's Assessment:
Project Planning: [Rating on a scale of 1-5]
Stakeholder Management: [Rating on a scale of 1-5]
Risk Assessment: [Rating on a scale of 1-5]
Gap Analysis:
Project Planning: [Identify the difference between self-assessment and manager's assessment]
Stakeholder Management: [Identify the difference between self-assessment and manager's assessment]
Risk Assessment: [Identify the difference between self-assessment and manager's assessment]
Analysis:
In this matrix, employees self-assess their skills, and managers provide their assessments. The gap analysis reveals areas where there is a significant difference between self-assessment and manager's assessment, indicating potential skill gaps.

3. Behavior Assessment:

Format: Behavioral Observation Checklist
Employee Name: [Insert Employee Name] Position: [Insert Employee Position] Date: [Insert Date]
Behavioral Observations:
☐ Punctuality and Attendance
☐ Team Collaboration
☐ Customer Interaction

☐ Problem-Solving
☐ Communication Skills

Observations and Feedback:

Punctuality and Attendance: [Manager's Observation and Feedback]

Team Collaboration: [Manager's Observation and Feedback]

Customer Interaction: [Manager's Observation and Feedback]

Problem-Solving: [Manager's Observation and Feedback]

Communication Skills: [Manager's Observation and Feedback]

Analysis:

In this checklist, a manager provides observations and feedback on various behaviors. This helps in identifying areas where behavioral improvements or training may be needed.

4. Attitude Assessment:

Format: Attitude Survey

Employee Name: [Insert Employee Name] Position: [Insert Employee Position] Date: [Insert Date]

Attitude Survey:

Customer-Centric Attitude: [Rating on a scale of 1-5]
Adaptability: [Rating on a scale of 1-5]
Teamwork: [Rating on a scale of 1-5]
Problem-Solving Attitude: [Rating on a scale of 1-5]
Positive Communication: [Rating on a scale of 1-5]

Additional Comments:

[Manager's comments or feedback on each attitude]

Analysis:

In this survey, employees rate themselves on various attitude dimensions, and managers provide comments or feedback. The analysis can reveal areas where attitude improvement or training is necessary.

These sample formats and examples provide a practical foundation for assessing training needs in areas such as product knowledge, skills, behavior, and attitude. Customizing these formats to suit your organization's specific needs and goals will enable you to conduct comprehensive training needs assessments effectively.

Selecting the Right Training Vendor

Selecting the right training vendor is a pivotal decision in the journey of implementing effective training programs. In this chapter, we will explore the intricacies of choosing a vendor, highlighting the critical criteria for evaluation, examining the significance of vendor reputation and track record, understanding the importance of customization capabilities, and navigating the delicate balance between cost and quality. By the end of this chapter, you will be well-equipped to make an informed choice that aligns with your organization's training objectives.

Vendor Evaluation Criteria

When considering potential training vendors, it's essential to establish a set of evaluation criteria. Here are the key steps:

- ✓ *Step 1: Define Your Requirements*
  Begin by defining your organization's specific training needs and objectives. What are you looking to achieve with the training program? Clear objectives will serve as a foundation for your evaluation criteria.
- ✓ *Step 2: Identify Potential Vendors*
  Research and compile a list of potential training vendors. This can include recommendations from industry peers, online searches, or RFP (Request for Proposal) submissions.
- ✓ *Step 3: Create a Vendor Evaluation Scorecard*
  Develop a vendor evaluation scorecard that includes criteria such as:

Experience and expertise in your industry
Range of training solutions offered
Quality of training materials and content
Cost-effectiveness
References and client testimonials
Ability to customize training programs
Track record of meeting deadlines
Responsiveness and communication

✓ *Step 4: Assign Weightage to Criteria*
Assign weightage to each criterion based on its importance to your organization. For example, if customization capabilities are a top priority, allocate a higher weight to this criterion in your scorecard.

✓ *Step 5: Evaluate and Score Vendors*
Engage with potential vendors, request proposals, and evaluate them based on your scorecard. Assign scores to each criterion and calculate the total scores for each vendor.

✓ *Step 6: Select the Vendor with the Highest Score*
The vendor with the highest score on your evaluation scorecard is typically the best fit for your organization's needs. However, consider conducting interviews or reference checks to gather additional insights before making a final decision.

Vendor Reputation and Track Record

The reputation and track record of a training vendor are paramount in your decision-making process. Here's how to assess this aspect:

✓ *Research Vendor Reputation*
Research the vendor's reputation in the industry by seeking feedback from current or

past clients, reading online reviews, and checking industry forums or associations.

✓ *Assess Track Record*
Review the vendor's track record by evaluating their history of successful training programs, on-time delivery, and client satisfaction. Request case studies or references to gain deeper insights.

✓ *Consider Industry Expertise*
Assess whether the vendor has specific expertise in your industry. Industry-specific knowledge can be valuable when tailoring training programs to your organization's unique needs.

Vendor Customization Capabilities

The ability to customize training programs to align with your organization's unique requirements is crucial. Here's how to evaluate a vendor's customization capabilities:

✓ *Define Customization Needs*
Clearly define your organization's customization needs. What aspects of the training program require customization, such as content, delivery methods, or assessment tools?

✓ *Request Customization Examples*
Ask potential vendors for examples of how they have customized training programs for other clients. These examples can demonstrate their ability to adapt to diverse needs.

✓ *Discuss Tailoring Processes*
✓ Engage in discussions with vendors about their processes for tailoring training programs.

Ensure they have a structured approach to customization that aligns with your objectives.

Cost vs. Quality Considerations

Balancing cost and quality is a delicate endeavor when selecting a training vendor. Here's how to strike that balance effectively:

- ✓ *Establish a Budget*
  Set a clear budget for your training program. Define the maximum amount you are willing to invest while considering the expected ROI.
- ✓ *Compare Costs Across Vendors*
  Request detailed cost proposals from potential vendors. Compare the costs against the quality of their training offerings and their ability to meet your objectives.
- ✓ *Consider Long-Term Value*
  Evaluate the long-term value of the training program. A slightly higher upfront cost may be justified if it leads to better training outcomes and ROI over time.
- ✓ *Negotiate*
  Engage in negotiations with the selected vendor to reach a cost agreement that aligns with your budget while maintaining the desired quality.

In conclusion, this chapter underscores the critical importance of selecting the right training vendor, a decision that can significantly impact the success of your training programs. By establishing clear evaluation criteria, assessing vendor reputation and track record, understanding customization capabilities, and carefully balancing cost and quality considerations, you can make an informed choice that advances your organization's training objectives.

Remember, the right vendor is not just a supplier but a partner in your journey to effective employee development.

Planning and Implementing Training Programs

Planning and implementing training programs is a critical phase in the journey of employee development. In this chapter, we will delve into the intricacies of crafting a training strategy, designing effective training modules, selecting appropriate delivery methods (whether in-person, virtual, or blended), and establishing mechanisms for monitoring and evaluating training programs. By the end of this chapter, you will be well-prepared to execute impactful training initiatives that drive growth and development within your organization.

Developing a Training Strategy

A well-defined training strategy serves as the roadmap for your organization's training initiatives. Here's how to develop a comprehensive training strategy:

- ✓ *Step 1: Assess Organizational Goals*
  Start by aligning your training strategy with the broader organizational goals. What are the key objectives you aim to achieve through training? For example, if your organization's goal is to expand market share, your training strategy may focus on sales and customer service training.

- ✓ *Step 2: Identify Target Audiences*
  Determine the specific employee groups or individuals who will benefit from the training. Consider their roles, skill levels, and training needs. A one-size-fits-all approach rarely yields optimal results.

✓ *Step 3: Define Learning Objectives*
Establish clear learning objectives for each training program. What should participants be able to do or understand after completing the training? Learning objectives provide a measurable framework for success.

✓ *Step 4: Design a Curriculum*
Develop a comprehensive curriculum that outlines the training content, sequence, and duration. Consider the use of various formats, including workshops, e-learning modules, and on-the-job training.

✓ *Step 5: Allocate Resources*
Allocate the necessary resources, including budget, trainers, materials, and technology, to support your training strategy effectively.

Designing Effective Training Modules
Effective training modules are the building blocks of successful training programs. Here's how to design modules that engage and educate participants:

✓ *Step 1: Define Module Objectives*
For each module within your training program, define clear objectives. What specific knowledge or skills should participants gain from this module?

✓ *Step 2: Structure Content Logically*
Organize module content in a logical and sequential manner. Start with foundational concepts and progressively move towards more complex topics.

✓ *Step 3: Utilize Active Learning Techniques*
Incorporate active learning techniques, such as case studies, group discussions, role-play

exercises, and simulations, to engage participants and promote skill development.
- ✓ *Step 4: Assess and Reinforce Learning*
  Include assessments within each module to gauge participant understanding. Use quizzes, practical exercises, or assignments to reinforce learning.
- ✓ *Step 5: Encourage Interactivity*
  Foster participant interaction by allowing questions, discussions, and feedback. Create a collaborative learning environment.

Delivery Methods: In-Person, Virtual, Blended

Selecting the right delivery method is crucial for effective training. Here are considerations for in-person, virtual, and blended training:
- ✓ *In-Person Training:*
  In-person training is highly interactive and suitable for hands-on skill development. It is ideal for scenarios like workshops, seminars, and on-site training. Ensure that training locations are accessible and conducive to learning.
- ✓ *Virtual Training:*
  Virtual training offers flexibility and cost-effectiveness. It is well-suited for remote teams or global organizations. Utilize video conferencing, e-learning platforms, and webinars to facilitate virtual training. Ensure that participants have the necessary technology and resources.
- ✓ *Blended Training:*
  Blended training combines both in-person and virtual elements. It provides the advantages of in-person interaction along with the flexibility

of virtual learning. Consider using in-person sessions for practical skills and virtual modules for theoretical knowledge.

Monitoring and Evaluating Training Programs

Monitoring and evaluating training programs are essential to ensure they meet their objectives and deliver a return on investment. Here's how to implement an effective monitoring and evaluation process:

- ✓ *Step 1: Define Key Performance Indicators (KPIs)*
  Establish KPIs that align with your training objectives. These may include improved job performance, increased sales, or enhanced customer satisfaction.
- ✓ *Step 2: Collect Data*
  Gather data before, during, and after the training program to assess its impact. This may include pre-training assessments, participant feedback, and post-training performance metrics.
- ✓ *Step 3: Evaluate Results*
  Analyze the collected data to evaluate the effectiveness of the training program. Compare post-training performance to pre-training benchmarks.
- ✓ *Step 4: Make Improvements*
  Based on the evaluation results, identify areas for improvement in both content and delivery. Continuous improvement ensures that training programs remain effective and relevant.
- ✓ *Step 5: Measure ROI*
  Calculate the return on investment (ROI) of the training program by comparing the

benefits (e.g., increased revenue or productivity) to the costs. A positive ROI demonstrates the program's value.

This chapter emphasizes the critical importance of planning and implementing training programs strategically. By developing a well-defined training strategy, designing effective training modules, selecting suitable delivery methods, and establishing robust monitoring and evaluation mechanisms, you can create training programs that drive growth, enhance employee skills, and contribute to the overall success of your organization. Remember, effective training is an ongoing process that adapts to the evolving needs of your workforce and industry.

Sample Formats of Planning and Implementing Training Programs

Developing a Training Strategy:
Format: Training Strategy Document
Training Strategy Document for Sales Team
1. Objective: To enhance the sales skills and product knowledge of the sales team, resulting in a 15% increase in sales revenue within six months.
2. Target Audience: Sales representatives, sales managers, and customer support staff.
3. Learning Objectives:
   - ✓ Improve product knowledge.
   - ✓ Enhance sales techniques.
   - ✓ Strengthen customer relationship management.
   - ✓ Boost negotiation skills.

Curriculum Outline:
Module 1: Product Knowledge (Duration: xx Days/Weeks)
Understanding product features and benefits.
Handling customer objections effectively.
Practical demonstrations and hands-on exercises.
Module 2: Sales Techniques (Duration: xx Days/Weeks)
Building rapport with clients.
Effective sales presentation and closing techniques.
Role-play exercises and real-world simulations.
Module 3: Customer Relationship Management (Duration: xx Days/Weeks)
Creating long-lasting customer relationships.
Handling customer feedback and complaints.

Case studies and group discussions.

Module 4: Negotiation Skills (Duration: xx Days/Weeks)

Mastering negotiation strategies.

Win-win negotiation approaches.

Mock negotiation sessions.

Resource Allocation:
- ✓ Budget: $XXXXX
- ✓ Trainers: Internal sales trainers and external sales experts.
- ✓ Training materials: Online courses, product manuals, and interactive software.

Designing Effective Training Modules:

Format: Training Module Outline

Training Module: Sales Presentation Skills

Module Objective: To equip sales representatives with effective sales presentation skills to improve customer engagement and increase conversion rates.

Module Content:

Part 1: Introduction to Sales Presentations (Duration: 2 hours)
- ✓ Understanding the importance of sales presentations.
- ✓ Elements of a successful sales presentation.
- ✓ Setting clear objectives for presentations.

Part 2: Structuring Your Presentation (Duration: 3 hours)
- ✓ Crafting a compelling opening.
- ✓ Building a persuasive narrative.
- ✓ Incorporating visuals and multimedia.
- ✓ Engaging the audience through storytelling.

Part 3: Delivery and Handling Questions (Duration: 2 hours)

- ✓ Effective communication techniques.
- ✓ Handling objections and questions gracefully.
- ✓ Building rapport during presentations.

Part 4: Practical Exercises (Duration: 2 hours)

- ✓ Role-play sessions for practicing presentation skills.
- ✓ Peer feedback and improvement suggestions.
- ✓ Assessment:

Each participant will deliver a sales presentation, which will be evaluated by trainers and peers.

Delivery Methods: In-Person, Virtual, Blended:
Format: Delivery Method Selection Matrix
Training Program: Leadership Development
Objective: To develop leadership skills among middle managers to improve team performance and innovation.

Delivery Methods:

- ✓ In-Person Sessions (25% of program)
  Leadership workshops held at regional offices.
  Hands-on team-building exercises.
  Opportunity for in-person networking and mentoring.
- ✓ Virtual Modules (50% of program)
  Online leadership courses accessible from anywhere.
  Virtual leadership coaching and feedback sessions.
  Webinars with guest speakers and leadership experts.
- ✓ Blended Approach (25% of program)
  In-person kickoff event to build rapport.
  Virtual modules for knowledge acquisition.
  In-person leadership project presentations and feedback sessions.

Monitoring and Evaluating Training Programs:
Format: Training Evaluation Plan
Training Evaluation Plan for Customer Service Training Program
Key Performance Indicators (KPIs):
- ✓ Increase in customer satisfaction ratings.
- ✓ Decrease in customer complaints.
- ✓ Improvement in first-call resolution rates.
- ✓ Post-training assessment scores.

Data Collection Methods:
- ✓ Pre-training and post-training customer satisfaction surveys.
- ✓ Customer feedback reports.
- ✓ Call center performance metrics.
- ✓ Employee assessments and quizzes.

Evaluation Process:
- ✓ Pre-training Customer Satisfaction Survey (Baseline): Conduct a survey to establish pre-training customer satisfaction levels.
- ✓ Post-training Customer Satisfaction Survey: After the training program, conduct a follow-up survey to measure changes in customer satisfaction.
- ✓ Monthly Review of Customer Complaints: Track and analyze customer complaints to identify trends and improvements.
- ✓ Call Center Performance Metrics: Monitor first-call resolution rates and customer interaction quality.
- ✓ Post-Training Employee Assessments: Evaluate the knowledge and skills of employees through post-training assessments.

Analysis and Improvement:
- ✓ Compare pre-training and post-training customer satisfaction scores.
- ✓ Address specific complaints and issues identified in customer feedback reports.
- ✓ Recognize improvements in call center performance metrics.
- ✓ Review employee assessment scores for any knowledge gaps and provide additional support as needed.

In conclusion, these sample formats and examples provide a practical foundation for planning and implementing training programs. Customizing these formats to align with your organization's specific training needs and goals will help you create effective and impactful training initiatives that yield positive results and contribute to the development of your workforce.

Measuring the Impact of Training

Effectively measuring the impact of training programs is a crucial aspect of talent development. It allows organizations to assess the return on investment (ROI), make data-driven decisions, and continuously improve their training efforts. In this chapter, we will explore comprehensive approaches to measuring training impact, including Kirkpatrick's Four Levels of Evaluation, the metrics for success, the significance of data-driven decision-making, and strategies for continuous improvement. By mastering these measurement techniques, you can optimize your training programs and achieve tangible results.

Kirkpatrick's Four Levels of Evaluation

Kirkpatrick's Four Levels of Evaluation is a widely recognized framework for assessing the effectiveness of training programs. Here's how to apply this model:

- ✓ *Step 1: Level 1 - Reaction*
  Gather feedback from participants to gauge their satisfaction with the training. Use surveys or interviews to collect their reactions and perceptions.
- ✓ *Step 2: Level 2 - Learning*
  Assess the extent to which participants have acquired new knowledge and skills. Administer quizzes, tests, or practical assessments to measure their learning outcomes.
- ✓ *Step 3: Level 3 - Behavior*
  Evaluate whether participants are applying what they learned in their actual work roles.

Observe their on-the-job performance and collect data on behavior changes.

✓ *Step 4: Level 4 - Results*
Determine the impact of training on broader organizational goals, such as increased sales, reduced errors, or improved customer satisfaction. Compare pre-training and post-training metrics to assess the ROI.

Example: A sales training program for a software company:

✓ Level 1: Participants complete a post-training survey, with 90% indicating high satisfaction.

✓ Level 2: Pre-training and post-training assessments show a 20% improvement in product knowledge.

✓ Level 3: Sales managers observe a 15% increase in the use of effective sales techniques.

✓ Level 4: Post-training, the company experiences a 25% boost in sales revenue.

Metrics for Success

To measure training impact effectively, identify and track key performance indicators (KPIs) aligned with your training objectives. Here's how to establish metrics for success:

✓ *Step 1: Define Clear Objectives*
Begin by defining specific training objectives. What outcomes do you expect from the training program? For example, if it's a leadership training program, objectives may include improved team productivity and reduced turnover.

✓ *Step 2: Identify Relevant Metrics*

Select KPIs that directly relate to your objectives. For leadership training, metrics could include employee engagement scores, leadership effectiveness assessments, or turnover rates among trained leaders.

✓ *Step 3: Establish Baselines*
Collect baseline data before implementing the training program to have a reference point for measuring change.

✓ *Step 4: Continuously Monitor Metrics*
Regularly track and monitor the selected metrics to assess the impact of training over time.

✓ *Step 5: Analyze and Adjust*
Analyze the data to determine if the training program is achieving the desired outcomes. If not, adjust the program and strategies accordingly.

Example: A customer service training program in a call center:

✓ Objective: Increase customer satisfaction.
✓ Metrics: Pre-training and post-training customer satisfaction scores.
✓ Baseline: Pre-training customer satisfaction score is 75.
✓ Monitoring: After six months, post-training customer satisfaction score increases to 85.

Data-Driven Decision Making

Data-driven decision-making relies on analyzing training data to inform strategic choices. Here's how to incorporate this approach:

✓ *Step 1: Collect Comprehensive Data*

Collect data at all levels of training evaluation, from reaction and learning to behavior and results.
- ✓ *Step 2: Analyze Data Holistically*
Combine data from different evaluation levels to gain a comprehensive view of training impact. Identify trends, patterns, and correlations.
- ✓ *Step 3: Use Data for Decision-Making*
Base decisions about training adjustments, resource allocation, and program improvements on the insights derived from data analysis.
- ✓ *Step 4: Communicate Findings*
Share the results and insights with relevant stakeholders, including training teams, management, and employees, to ensure alignment and transparency.

Example: An IT company analyzes data from a cyber-security training program:

Data reveals that employees who completed the training are less likely to fall victim to phishing attacks.

The company allocates additional resources to expand the training program, targeting all employees to enhance cyber-security awareness.

Continuous Improvement Strategies

To continuously improve training programs, organizations must embrace a culture of ongoing enhancement. Here are strategies for achieving this:
- ✓ *Step 1: Collect Feedback*
Regularly seek feedback from participants, trainers, and stakeholders to identify areas for improvement.

✓ *Step 2: Conduct Post-Training Assessments*
Administer post-training assessments to evaluate learning outcomes and identify knowledge gaps.
✓ *Step 3: Evaluate Training Materials*
Review training materials and content regularly to ensure they remain relevant and up-to-date.
✓ *Step 4: Adapt to Changing Needs*
Adapt training programs to address evolving organizational needs and industry trends.

Example: An engineering firm gathers feedback from participants after each technical training session. Based on this feedback, they regularly update training materials to align with the latest industry standards and technology advancements.

In conclusion, this chapter underscores the critical importance of measuring the impact of training programs. By applying Kirkpatrick's Four Levels of Evaluation, defining relevant metrics for success, embracing data-driven decision-making, and continually improving training strategies, organizations can ensure that their training efforts yield measurable results and contribute to the achievement of broader organizational goals. The ability to measure and adapt training programs is essential for staying competitive and nurturing a culture of ongoing learning and development.

Sample Formats for Measuring the Impact of Training

Here are sample formats and detailed examples for each of the aspects covered in the earlier chapter:

1. Kirkpatrick's Four Levels of Evaluation:
Format: Evaluation Report

Training Program Evaluation Report

Objective: To assess the impact of the "Leadership Development Program" on participants and the organization.

Level 1 - Reaction:
- ✓ Participant Satisfaction: 92% of participants reported high satisfaction with the program.
- ✓ Post-training Survey Feedback: Positive feedback regarding the quality of trainers and content.

Level 2 - Learning:
- ✓ Pre-training vs. Post-training Knowledge Assessment:
  Pre-training average score: 65%
  Post-training average score: 85%
- ✓ Skill Assessment: Demonstrated a 20% improvement in leadership skills, as assessed by trainers.

Level 3 - Behavior:
- ✓ On-the-Job Observations: Supervisors observed that program participants consistently applied leadership principles and improved team collaboration.
- ✓ Peer Feedback: Colleagues noted increased confidence and effective communication among program participants.

Level 4 - Results:

- ✓ Organizational Performance Metrics: Employee Engagement: Improved by 12%.
- ✓ Turnover Rate among teams led by program participants: Decreased by 10%.
- ✓ Productivity Metrics: Showed a 15% increase in team output.

2. Metrics for Success: Format: Metrics Dashboard

Training Impact Metrics Dashboard

Objective: To measure the effectiveness of the "Sales Training Program" in achieving its objectives.

Metrics:

Objective 1: Increase Sales Revenue

- ✓ Pre-training vs. Post-training Sales Revenue Comparison
- ✓ Baseline Sales Revenue: $500,000
- ✓ Post-training Sales Revenue: $600,000
- ✓ Percentage Increase: 20%

Objective 2: Improve Customer Satisfaction

- ✓ Pre-training vs. Post-training Customer Satisfaction Scores
- ✓ Baseline Customer Satisfaction Score: 75
- ✓ Post-training Customer Satisfaction Score: 85
- ✓ Percentage Increase: 13%

Objective 3: Enhance Product Knowledge

- ✓ Pre-training vs. Post-training Product Knowledge Assessment
- ✓ Pre-training Average Score: 60%
- ✓ Post-training Average Score: 90%
- ✓ Percentage Increase: 50%

3. Data-Driven Decision Making: Format: Decision-Making Report

Data-Driven Decision-Making Report

Objective: To make data-informed decisions regarding the "Customer Service Training Program."

Data Sources:
- ✓ Post-training Customer Feedback Surveys
- ✓ Customer Service Performance Metrics
- ✓ Employee Performance Metrics

Analysis:
- ✓ Analysis of customer feedback reveals that customers are more satisfied with the responsiveness and problem-solving skills of trained customer service representatives.
- ✓ Employee performance metrics show a noticeable decrease in average handling time for customer inquiries among trained representatives.

Decision: Based on the data, the organization decides to expand the training program to include all customer service teams, aiming to achieve similar improvements in customer satisfaction and employee performance across the board.

4. Continuous Improvement Strategies: *Format: Improvement Plan*

Continuous Improvement Plan for the "Technical Skills Training Program"

Objective: To continuously enhance the effectiveness of the training program.

Steps:

Collecting Participant Feedback
- ✓ Conduct regular surveys after each training session to gather feedback on content, trainers, and overall experience.
- ✓ Feedback will be analyzed to identify areas for improvement.

Post-Training Assessments

- ✓ Administer post-training assessments to measure the retention and application of technical skills.
- ✓ Identify knowledge gaps and adjust training content accordingly.

Content Review

- ✓ Review training materials and update them to reflect the latest industry standards and technological advancements.
- ✓ Ensure that content remains relevant and up-to-date.

Adaptation to Industry Trends

- ✓ Stay updated on industry trends and emerging technologies.
- ✓ Adapt the training program to incorporate relevant trends and technologies as needed.

Example: After analyzing feedback from participants and conducting post-training assessments, the training program for software developers identified a need for updated content on a new programming language. The program adjusted its curriculum to include this language, ensuring that participants remained current with industry trends.

Legal and Ethical Considerations in Training

In today's corporate landscape, training programs must not only be effective but also legally and ethically sound. In this chapter, we delve into the critical aspects of legal and ethical considerations in training, covering compliance and regulatory training, diversity, equity, and inclusion (DEI) training, privacy and data security concerns, and the protection of intellectual property related to training content. Understanding and navigating these issues is essential to creating training programs that align with both legal requirements and ethical standards.

Compliance and Regulatory Training

Compliance and regulatory training is vital for organizations to ensure that their employees adhere to legal requirements and industry-specific regulations. Here's how to approach it:

- ✓ *Step 1: Identify Applicable Regulations*
  Determine which regulations are relevant to your industry and organization. This may include laws related to safety, finance, healthcare, or data privacy.
- ✓ *Step 2: Create Comprehensive Training Content*
  Develop training content that covers all relevant regulations. This content should be easy to understand and tailored to your organization's specific needs.
- ✓ *Step 3: Delivery and Tracking*
  Deliver the training to all relevant employees and track their completion. Use learning

management systems (LMS) to document training records.

- ✓ *Step 4: Regular Updates and Assessments*
  Regularly update training materials to reflect changes in regulations. Conduct assessments to ensure employees understand and can apply the regulations in their roles.

Example: A financial institution provides annual compliance training to employees to ensure they understand the latest financial regulations and can prevent fraudulent activities. The training covers topics such as anti-money laundering (AML) laws and consumer protection regulations.

Diversity, Equity, and Inclusion (DEI) Training

DEI training is essential for promoting a diverse and inclusive workplace. Here's how to approach it:

- ✓ *Step 1: Assess Organizational Needs*
  Conduct an assessment to understand the specific DEI needs and challenges within your organization. Identify areas where training can make a difference.
- ✓ *Step 2: Design Inclusive Content*
  Develop training content that addresses bias, stereotypes, and promotes inclusive behaviors. Ensure that the training is engaging and relevant to all employees.
- ✓ *Step 3: Facilitate Open Discussions*
  Encourage open and respectful discussions during DEI training sessions. Create a safe space for employees to share their experiences and perspectives.
- ✓ *Step 4: Monitor Progress*

Regularly monitor DEI efforts, collect feedback from participants, and assess the impact of training on workplace diversity and inclusion.

Example: An IT company conducts DEI training that includes modules on unconscious bias, cultural sensitivity, and inclusive leadership. Through these sessions, employees learn to recognize and challenge biases, creating a more inclusive workplace.

Privacy and Data Security

Privacy and data security are paramount, especially when dealing with employee data and training records. Here's how to address these concerns:

- ✓ *Secure Data Storage*
  Ensure that all employee training records and data are securely stored. Implement encryption and access controls to protect sensitive information.
- ✓ *Obtain Consent*
  Obtain clear consent from employees for collecting and using their training data. Explain how their data will be used and stored.
- ✓ *Compliance with Data Regulations*
  Comply with data protection regulations such as GDPR (General Data Protection Regulation) or HIPAA (Health Insurance Portability and Accountability Act) if applicable to your organization/country.
- ✓ *Regular Data Audits*
  Conduct regular audits to ensure that data security protocols are in place and being followed. Address any vulnerabilities promptly.

Example: A healthcare organization collects and stores training records of medical staff. They ensure that all data is encrypted, access is restricted to authorized personnel, and employees are informed about the use of their data for compliance and training purposes.

Intellectual Property and Training Content

Protecting intellectual property related to training content is essential. Here's how to safeguard it:

- ✓ *Define Ownership*
  Clearly define who owns the intellectual property rights to training materials. Typically, the organization or its training team holds these rights.
- ✓ *Copyright and Licensing*
  Apply copyrights to training content and clearly state the terms of use and distribution. Consider licensing arrangements for third-party content.
- ✓ *Protect Trade Secrets*
  If your training content includes proprietary methods or trade secrets, take measures to protect them from unauthorized disclosure.
- ✓ *Non-disclosure Agreements (NDAs)*
  When collaborating with external training providers or contractors, use non-disclosure agreements to ensure they respect your intellectual property.

Example: An automotive manufacturer creates a comprehensive training program for its production processes. They copyright the training materials and include non-disclosure clauses in contracts with training vendors to safeguard their intellectual property.

In conclusion, this chapter underscores the significance of legal and ethical considerations in training programs. By addressing compliance and regulatory training, promoting diversity, equity, and inclusion, ensuring privacy and data security, and protecting intellectual property, organizations can develop training initiatives that not only enhance employee skills but also adhere to legal requirements and ethical standards. This comprehensive approach ensures that training programs are not only effective but also aligned with the organization's legal and ethical obligations.

Common Challenges Managers Encounter during Training Initiatives

Let's explore some common challenges that managers might encounter during training initiatives and provide practical solutions and strategies for overcoming them:

Challenge 1: Resistance to Change

Solution: When employees resist training or change, it's essential to communicate the benefits clearly. Highlight how the training will improve their skills, job satisfaction, and career growth. Engage employees early in the planning process, seeking their input and addressing concerns.

Challenge 2: Limited Budget

Solution: To overcome budget constraints, prioritize training needs based on organizational goals. Explore cost-effective training methods, such as e-learning or blended learning. Seek external funding sources or grants, and consider leveraging free or low-cost online resources.

Challenge 3: Lack of Engagement

Solution: Make training engaging by incorporating interactive elements like quizzes, discussions, and hands-on exercises. Use real-life scenarios and case studies relevant to participants' roles. Encourage peer learning and provide opportunities for feedback.

Challenge 4: Measuring Training Effectiveness

Solution: To measure training impact, use a combination of quantitative and qualitative methods. Implement Kirkpatrick's Four Levels of Evaluation, including reaction, learning, behavior, and results assessments. Collect feedback from participants, supervisors, and stakeholders.

Challenge 5: Maintaining Consistency
Solution: To ensure consistent training across the organization, create standardized training materials and modules. Implement a Learning Management System (LMS) for easy access to training content. Train trainers and facilitators to deliver content uniformly.

Challenge 6: Time Constraints
Solution: Recognize employees' time constraints and offer flexible training options. Use microlearning modules for quick, bite-sized training sessions. Allow self-paced learning and provide on-the-job training opportunities.

Challenge 7: Resistance to Technology
Solution: Address technology resistance through comprehensive user training. Offer user-friendly platforms and provide step-by-step guides. Encourage peer support and create a culture of tech proficiency.

Challenge 8: Adapting to Remote Work
Solution: In remote work scenarios, emphasize virtual training options. Use video conferencing, webinars, and virtual simulations for interactive learning. Ensure training materials are accessible remotely.

Challenge 9: Identifying Training Needs Accurately
Solution: Conduct a thorough needs assessment to identify training gaps accurately. Use surveys, interviews, and performance data. Involve managers and supervisors in identifying team-specific training needs.

Challenge 10: Sustaining a Learning Culture
Solution: Foster a learning culture by integrating training into daily workflows. Encourage continuous

learning through mentorship, peer support, and recognition. Celebrate successes and showcase the benefits of learning and development.

Challenge 11: Tracking Training Progress

Solution: Implement a robust tracking system or Learning Management System (LMS) to monitor training progress. Use analytics to assess completion rates, quiz scores, and learner engagement. Provide regular progress reports to managers and employees.

Challenge 12: Resistance from Senior Leadership

Solution: To gain support from senior leadership, align training initiatives with strategic organizational goals. Emphasize the potential for ROI and improved performance. Provide data-driven evidence of training effectiveness.

By addressing these common challenges with practical solutions and strategies, managers can navigate training initiatives more effectively, ensuring that they deliver maximum value to both the organization and its employees.

Steps a Training Manager/ Trainer Undertakes to Remain Effective and Up-to-date

Prioritizing Continuous Learning and Professional Growth

1. Stay Current in the Field: Regularly read industry publications, blogs, and books related to training and development. Attend conferences, seminars, and webinars to learn about the latest trends and innovations.

2. Seek Professional Development: Pursue relevant certifications or advanced degrees in training and development. Participate in workshops or courses that focus on instructional design, learning technology, or other related skills.

3. Network and Collaborate: Join professional associations such as ATD (Association for Talent Development) or SHRM (Society for Human Resource Management) or other such bodies in your respective countries to connect with peers and access resources. Collaborate with colleagues and attend networking events to exchange ideas and best practices.

4. Engage in Self-Assessment: Regularly assess your own training skills and knowledge gaps. Solicit feedback from participants and colleagues to identify areas for improvement.

5. Experiment with New Approaches: Embrace innovative training methods such as micro-learning, gamification, and virtual reality to keep training content engaging and effective. Experiment with new

tools and technologies that can enhance the learning experience.

6. Incorporate Feedback: Use evaluations and feedback from training sessions to refine and improve your training materials and delivery methods. Encourage open communication with participants to understand their needs and preferences.

7. Mentorship and Coaching: Seek mentorship from experienced trainers or training managers. Consider becoming a mentor to junior trainers to reinforce your own understanding of training concepts.

8. Stay Tech-Savvy: Keep up with technological advancements relevant to training, such as learning management systems (LMS), e-learning platforms, and virtual classrooms. Leverage online courses and tutorials to enhance your tech skills.

9. Conduct Research: Conduct research on industry-specific training needs and best practices. Stay informed about changes in laws, regulations, and compliance requirements related to training.

10. Set Personal Goals: Define clear learning and development goals for yourself, such as mastering a new training methodology or achieving a specific certification. Create a personalized learning plan with milestones and timelines.

11. Evaluate Training Impact: Regularly assess the impact of your training programs on participants' skills and performance. Use data and metrics to measure success and identify areas for improvement.

12. Reflect and Adapt: Reflect on your training experiences and adapt your approach based on lessons learned. Be open to change and willing to adjust your methods as needed.

13. Practice Self-Care: Maintain a healthy work-life balance to prevent burnout and maintain enthusiasm for training. Prioritize self-care practices, including exercise, mindfulness, and relaxation techniques.
14. Stay Ethical and Inclusive: Stay updated on ethical considerations in training, including diversity and inclusion best practices. Ensure that your training materials and methods align with ethical standards.

By consistently pursuing these steps, training managers and trainers can not only remain effective and up-to-date but also contribute significantly to the professional development and success of their organizations.

Creating a Culture of Continuous Learning

In today's dynamic and ever-evolving work environment, fostering a culture of continuous learning is no longer a mere aspiration but a necessity. In this chapter, we will explore the essential elements of cultivating a learning-centric workplace, including strategies to foster a learning culture, methods for nurturing career development and growth, the importance of feedback and employee input, and techniques to encourage self-directed learning. By the end of this chapter, you will be well-prepared to transform your organization into a hub of ongoing learning and development.

Fostering a Learning Culture

Creating a learning culture is about instilling a mindset that values continuous learning as a cornerstone of personal and organizational growth. Here's how to foster such a culture:

- ✓ *Set a Clear Vision*
  Define and communicate a clear vision of the organization's commitment to continuous learning. Leaders must champion this vision and actively participate in learning initiatives.
- ✓ *Align Learning with Goals*
  Ensure that learning goals align with broader organizational objectives. This demonstrates the tangible impact of learning on the organization's success.
- ✓ *Provide Learning Resources*
  Invest in resources that support learning, such as training programs, e-learning platforms,

books, and access to experts. Make these resources readily available to employees.
✓ *Encourage Knowledge Sharing*
Promote a culture of knowledge sharing where employees freely exchange information, insights, and best practices. Establish platforms for collaboration and discussion.

Example: A technology company dedicates time during weekly team meetings for knowledge sharing sessions. Team members share recent discoveries, lessons learned, and industry trends.

Career Development and Growth

Career development and growth opportunities are powerful drivers of employee engagement and retention. Here's how to nurture them:
✓ *Step 1: Identify Career Paths*
Work with employees to identify potential career paths within the organization. Discuss aspirations, strengths, and areas for development.
✓ *Step 2: Create Individual Development Plans*
Collaboratively develop individualized development plans for each employee. These plans should include specific goals, skills to acquire, and timelines.
✓ *Step 3: Offer Skill-Building Opportunities*
Provide access to skill-building opportunities such as workshops, courses, mentorship programs, and stretch assignments.
✓ *Step 4: Regularly Review Progress*
Schedule regular check-ins to review progress and adjust development plans as needed. Ensure that employees feel supported in their growth journey.

Example: A manufacturing company offers a mentorship program where junior employees are paired with experienced mentors. The program includes regular meetings to discuss career goals and development.

Feedback and Employee Input

Feedback and employee input are vital for maintaining a learning culture. Here's how to incorporate them:

- ✓ *Open Channels of Communication*
  Establish open and transparent channels for employees to provide feedback and share ideas. This can include suggestion boxes, regular surveys, or one-on-one discussions.
- ✓ *Act on Feedback*
  Demonstrate a commitment to acting on feedback by implementing relevant suggestions and addressing concerns promptly.
- ✓ *Encourage Peer Feedback*
  Promote a culture of peer feedback where employees provide constructive input to help each other grow. Provide guidelines for giving and receiving feedback.
- ✓ *Recognize and Celebrate Contributions*
  Acknowledge and celebrate employee contributions to learning and development initiatives. This reinforces the value of their input.

Example: A software development company conducts anonymous quarterly surveys to gather feedback on training programs. They use this feedback to make improvements and share updates with employees.

Encouraging Self-Directed Learning
Self-directed learning empowers employees to take ownership of their development. Here's how to encourage it:

- ✓ *Communicate the Importance*
  Highlight the benefits of self-directed learning, such as personal growth, increased job satisfaction, and career advancement.
- ✓ *Provide Learning Resources*
  Offer a variety of resources, such as online courses, books, articles, and webinars that employees can access independently.
- ✓ *Set Learning Goals*
  Encourage employees to set their own learning goals and objectives. These should align with their interests and career aspirations.
- ✓ *Support and Recognize Efforts*
  Provide support, including time and resources, for self-directed learning endeavors. Recognize and reward employees who actively pursue self-improvement.

Example: An advertising agency encourages self-directed learning by providing a learning stipend for each employee. This stipend can be used to enroll in courses, attend conferences, or purchase books related to their field.

In conclusion, this chapter underscores the significance of creating a culture of continuous learning within your organization. By fostering a learning-centric environment, nurturing career development and growth, actively seeking feedback and input from employees, and promoting self-directed learning, you can empower your workforce to adapt and thrive in a rapidly changing world.

Embracing continuous learning not only benefits individual employees but also positions your organization for long-term success and innovation.

Training in the Future: Emerging Trends

The landscape of employee training is constantly evolving, and to stay competitive and relevant, organizations must adapt to emerging trends. In this chapter, we will explore the future of training, including technology-driven solutions, the rise of micro-learning and on-demand training, the impact of gamification on employee engagement, and the potential of adaptive learning and personalization. By embracing these trends, you can position your organization at the forefront of employee development, ensuring a skilled and motivated workforce.

Technology-Driven Training Solutions
The integration of technology into training has transformed the way employees acquire knowledge and skills. Here's how to harness technology-driven training solutions:

- ✓ *Step 1: Identify Technology Needs*
  Assess your organization's training needs and identify areas where technology can enhance the learning experience. This may include e-learning platforms, virtual reality (VR), or augmented reality (AR) applications.
- ✓ *Step 2: Select the Right Technology*
  Choose technology that aligns with your training goals. For example, if you want to provide hands-on experience, VR simulations can be highly effective. Ensure that the technology is user-friendly and accessible to all employees.

✓ *Step 3: Develop Interactive Content*
Create engaging and interactive content that leverages technology. Use multimedia, simulations, and quizzes to make learning more dynamic and effective.
✓ *Step 4: Measure and Analyze*
Utilize analytics tools to track learner progress and engagement. Analyze data to identify areas for improvement and tailor training content accordingly.

Example: A retail company implements a mobile app that allows employees to access bite-sized training videos on their smartphones. The app tracks progress, provides instant feedback, and offers quizzes to reinforce learning.

Micro-learning and On-Demand Training

Micro-learning and on-demand training are gaining prominence due to their flexibility and efficiency. Here's how to incorporate these approaches:

✓ *Break Down Content*
Divide training content into small, digestible modules. Each module should focus on a specific topic or skill.
✓ *Create a Learning Library*
Build a learning library that employees can access anytime, anywhere. Ensure that the content is easily searchable and available on various devices.
✓ *Promote Self-Directed Learning*
Encourage employees to take ownership of their learning by allowing them to choose when and what they want to learn. Provide incentives for completing modules.

Example: A software company offers a library of short video tutorials on coding techniques. Developers can access these tutorials whenever they encounter specific coding challenges, enabling just-in-time learning.

Gamification and Employee Engagement
Gamification infuses training with elements of gaming, enhancing engagement and motivation. Here's how to implement gamification effectively:
- ✓ *Step 1: Set Clear Objectives*
  Define specific learning objectives and outcomes that you want to achieve through gamification.
- ✓ *Step 2: Design Game Elements*
  Incorporate game elements such as points, badges, leaderboards, and rewards into your training programs.
- ✓ *Step 3: Create Engaging Scenarios*
  Develop scenarios and challenges that mirror real-world situations. Encourage healthy competition among learners.
- ✓ *Step 4: Monitor Progress*
  Track learners' progress and provide immediate feedback. Celebrate achievements and milestones.

Example: A customer service training program includes a simulated customer service game where employees must resolve customer inquiries within a set time frame. High performers earn badges and recognition.

Adaptive Learning and Personalization
Adaptive learning tailors training to individual learners, optimizing the learning experience. Here's

how to implement adaptive learning and personalization:

✓ *Step 1: Assess Learner Proficiency*
Use pre-assessments to gauge learners' existing knowledge and skills. This helps determine their starting point.

✓ *Step 2: Customize Learning Paths*
Based on assessment results, create customized learning paths for each learner. Beginners and advanced learners follow different routes.

✓ *Step 3: Provide Real-Time Feedback*
Offer immediate feedback and support as learners progress through the training program. Adjust content and difficulty levels as needed.

✓ *Step 4: Continuously Update Content*
Regularly update training content to reflect changes in skills and knowledge requirements.

Example: An IT certification program uses adaptive learning to assess candidates' technical skills. Depending on their initial proficiency, candidates receive customized study materials and practice tests to help them prepare effectively.

In conclusion, this chapter explores the future of training, highlighting the transformative impact of technology-driven solutions, microlearning, gamification, and adaptive learning. Embracing these trends can elevate your training programs, making them more engaging, efficient, and personalized.

By staying ahead of these emerging trends, your organization can ensure that its workforce remains adaptable, skilled, and motivated in the ever-evolving business landscape.

International Perspectives on Training- Cultural Differences and Global Best Practices

This section can be valuable for organizations with a global workforce.

International Perspectives on Training: Bridging Cultural Differences

In today's interconnected world, many organizations operate on a global scale, and their workforces span diverse cultures, languages, and backgrounds. To effectively train employees across borders and ensure consistent development, it's essential to consider international perspectives on training. This entails understanding and addressing cultural differences while embracing global best practices in learning and development.

Cultural Differences in Training:
- ✓ **Communication Styles:** Different cultures have varying communication norms. Some cultures prioritize direct and explicit communication, while others favor indirect or nuanced communication. Training materials and facilitation should align with the communication preferences of the target audience.
- ✓ **Hierarchy and Authority:** Hierarchical structures and authority dynamics differ across cultures. In some cultures, questioning authority may be discouraged, while others encourage open dialogue. Trainers should be

aware of these dynamics and create a safe and inclusive learning environment.

- ✓ **Learning Styles:** Cultural factors can influence how individuals prefer to learn. For example, some cultures value group learning and collaboration, while others emphasize individual self-study. Training programs should incorporate a mix of learning approaches to accommodate diverse preferences.
- ✓ **Feedback Culture:** The way feedback is given and received can vary greatly between cultures. Some cultures may view constructive criticism positively, while others may find it uncomfortable. Trainers should adapt feedback delivery to align with cultural norms.
- ✓ **Time Orientation:** Cultural attitudes toward time, punctuality, and deadlines can differ significantly. Training schedules and expectations should be flexible enough to accommodate varying time orientations.

Global Best Practices in Training:
- ✓ **Cultural Sensitivity Training:** Incorporate cultural sensitivity and diversity training into your programs. Teach employees about cultural differences, biases, and the importance of inclusion.
- ✓ **Multilingual Training:** If your workforce spans multiple languages, provide training materials in the native languages of participants. Multilingual training fosters a sense of inclusivity and accessibility.
- ✓ **Cross-Cultural Communication Skills:** Offer training modules that focus on cross-cultural communication skills, helping employees

navigate diverse work environments effectively.
- ✓ **Virtual Learning Platforms:** Leverage technology to facilitate virtual training and collaboration among global teams. Virtual platforms can bridge geographical gaps and promote knowledge sharing.
- ✓ **Global Mentoring and Coaching Programs:** Implement mentoring and coaching programs that pair employees from different regions. These programs promote cross-cultural understanding and skill development.
- ✓ **Global Leadership Development:** Develop leadership programs that prepare leaders to manage diverse teams effectively. Global leaders should be equipped with cross-cultural leadership skills.
- ✓ **Localized Content:** Customize training content to make it culturally relevant while ensuring alignment with global organizational goals.
- ✓ **Feedback Mechanisms:** Establish feedback mechanisms that allow employees to provide input on training programs. This ensures that training remains relevant and culturally sensitive.

Benefits of Embracing International Perspectives:
- ✓ **Enhanced Cultural Competence:** Employees develop a deeper understanding and respect for cultural differences, fostering a more inclusive and harmonious work environment.

- ✓ **Increased Global Competitiveness:** Organizations that embrace international perspectives are better equipped to compete in global markets, as they can adapt more easily to local customs and market trends.
- ✓ **Improved Employee Engagement:** Employees appreciate organizations that invest in their cultural development. Engaged employees are more likely to stay with the company and contribute positively to its success.
- ✓ **Global Talent Development:** Organizations can identify and nurture talent from diverse regions, harnessing the full potential of their global workforce.

In conclusion, international perspectives on training are invaluable for organizations with a global presence. By recognizing and respecting cultural differences while embracing global best practices, organizations can create a learning and development environment that fosters inclusivity, cultural competence, and global competitiveness. This approach not only benefits the organization but also enriches the experiences of its employees around the world.

Case Studies of Successful Training Programs

In this chapter, we will explore real-world case studies of successful training programs implemented by organizations to achieve specific goals and address unique challenges. These case studies illustrate the practical application of the principles and strategies discussed throughout this book, providing valuable insights into the planning, execution, and outcomes of these training initiatives.

Case Study 1: Transforming Customer Service through Training

Background: Company A, a retail chain, faced declining customer satisfaction scores and an increase in customer complaints. They identified a need to revamp their customer service approach and decided to implement a comprehensive training program.

Steps Taken:

- ✓ *Step 1: Needs Assessment*
  Company A conducted a thorough needs assessment, which included customer feedback, employee surveys, and mystery shopper evaluations. They identified communication skills, product knowledge, and conflict resolution as areas requiring improvement.

- ✓ *Step 2: Customized Training Content*
  Based on the needs assessment, the training team developed customized content that included modules on active listening, empathy, product knowledge, and de-escalation techniques.

✓ *Step 3: Delivery and Engagement*
The training program was delivered in a blended format, combining in-person workshops with e-learning modules. Interactive activities, role-plays, and simulations were incorporated to engage participants.

✓ *Step 4: Monitoring and Feedback*
Company A monitored the program's progress by tracking key performance indicators (KPIs), such as customer satisfaction scores and the number of customer complaints. They also gathered feedback from participants and adjusted the training based on their input.

Results:

✓ Within six months of implementing the training program, customer satisfaction scores increased by 20%.

✓ The number of customer complaints decreased by 30%.

✓ Employees reported feeling more confident in handling customer interactions.

Case Study 2: Building Leadership Capabilities

Background: Company B, a technology firm, recognized the need to develop strong leadership within its organization to drive innovation and employee engagement. They aimed to build leadership capabilities from within.

Steps Taken:

✓ *Step 1: Leadership Competency Assessment*
Company B conducted a leadership competency assessment to identify areas where leaders needed development. They found that while technical skills were strong,

soft skills like communication and team leadership needed improvement.

✓ *Step 2: Leadership Development Program*
Based on the assessment, Company B designed a year-long leadership development program. The program included modules on emotional intelligence, effective communication, conflict resolution, and strategic thinking.

✓ *Step 3: Mentorship and Coaching*
Participants in the program were paired with experienced mentors who provided guidance and coaching. Regular one-on-one coaching sessions helped participants apply what they learned in real work situations.

✓ *Step 4: Measuring Impact*
Company B regularly measured the impact of the program through 360-degree feedback, employee engagement surveys, and leadership effectiveness assessments.

Results:

✓ Over two years, the organization saw a 15% increase in employee engagement scores.

✓ Leadership effectiveness, as assessed by employees, improved by 25%.

✓ Several program participants were promoted to higher leadership positions within the company.

Case Study 3: Navigating Change with Employee Training

Background: Company C, a manufacturing company, was undergoing a significant technology overhaul, introducing automation and new processes. They recognized the need to train employees to adapt to these changes.

Steps Taken:

- ✓ *Step 1: Change Readiness Assessment*
  Company C conducted a change readiness assessment to gauge employees' readiness for the upcoming changes. They identified areas of resistance and uncertainty.
- ✓ *Step 2: Change Management Training*
  The organization developed a change management training program that focused on helping employees embrace change, adapt to new technologies, and acquire the necessary skills.
- ✓ *Step 3: Hands-On Training and Simulation*
  To ensure practical understanding, Company C conducted hands-on training sessions and simulations where employees could practice new processes and use new tools.
- ✓ *Step 4: Post-Implementation Support*
  After the technology overhaul, the organization provided ongoing support through mentorship programs and additional training sessions to address any challenges that arose.

Results:

- ✓ The transition to new technology was smoother, with minimal disruptions to production.
- ✓ Employee morale remained high, and resistance to change decreased significantly.
- ✓ Productivity increased by 20% as employees adapted to more efficient processes.

In conclusion, these case studies demonstrate the successful application of training strategies to address real-world challenges and achieve specific organizational goals. Whether it's transforming customer service, building leadership capabilities, or navigating change, effective training programs play a pivotal role in enhancing employee skills, improving performance, and ultimately driving organizational success.

Case Studies from Various Industries

Case Study 1: Healthcare Industry - Improving Patient Care through Training

Background: A large hospital network faced challenges related to patient satisfaction and safety. To address these issues, they initiated a comprehensive training program.

Training Objectives:
- ✓ Enhance patient care skills of nurses and medical staff.
- ✓ Improve communication among healthcare teams.
- ✓ Ensure compliance with healthcare regulations.

Training Approach:
- ✓ Conducted in-person workshops and simulations for hands-on practice.
- ✓ Included modules on effective communication, patient empathy, and compliance.
- ✓ Utilized role-play scenarios to simulate real-life healthcare situations.

Results:
- ✓ Patient satisfaction scores improved by 25%.
- ✓ Medical staff reported increased confidence in handling complex cases.
- ✓ A decrease in medical errors and improved compliance with healthcare regulations.

Case Study 2: Manufacturing Industry - Increasing Efficiency and Safety

Background: A manufacturing company faced challenges related to operational efficiency and workplace safety. They initiated a training program to address these issues.

Training Objectives:
- ✓ Improve machine operation skills.
- ✓ Enhance safety awareness among employees.
- ✓ Reduce accidents and downtime.

Training Approach:
- ✓ Developed interactive e-learning modules on machine operation and safety.
- ✓ Conducted regular safety drills and emergency response training.
- ✓ Implemented a rewards system for employees who demonstrated exemplary safety practices.

Results:
- ✓ Reduced workplace accidents by 30%.
- ✓ Increased machine uptime and overall efficiency.
- ✓ Improved employee morale and engagement.

Case Study 3: Information Technology (IT) Industry - Leadership Development

Background: An IT services company aimed to develop strong leadership within its organization to drive innovation and client satisfaction. They initiated a leadership development program.

Training Objectives:
- ✓ Build leadership capabilities.
- ✓ Foster a culture of innovation and client-centricity.
- ✓ Enhance project management and client communication skills.

Training Approach:
- ✓ Implemented a year-long leadership development program.

- ✓ Included modules on emotional intelligence, client engagement, and project management.
- ✓ Provided one-on-one coaching and mentoring for program participants.

Results:

- ✓ Increased client satisfaction scores by 20%.
- ✓ Improved leadership effectiveness, as assessed by employees.
- ✓ Several program participants were promoted to higher leadership positions.

These case studies demonstrate how training principles can be applied effectively across different industries to address specific challenges and achieve organizational objectives. They highlight the versatility and impact of well-designed training programs in various contexts.

Formats and Samples of Other Assessments and Forms

Sample Training Needs Assessment Questionnaires

A well-designed training needs assessment questionnaire is crucial for identifying gaps in knowledge, skills, behavior, and attitude. Below is a sample format for a training needs assessment questionnaire. This sample questionnaire is a starting point for assessing training needs. Organizations can customize it to suit their specific industry and training objectives.

Training Needs Assessment Questionnaire

Instructions: Please answer the following questions to help us understand your training needs better. Your responses will remain confidential.

1. Personal Information:

Name:

Department/Team:

Job Title:

Length of Employment:

2. Training Experience:

Have you participated in any training programs within the past year? (Yes/No)

If yes, please list the training programs:

3. Skills and Knowledge:

Please rate your current proficiency level (1 = Not proficient, 5 = Very proficient) in the following areas:

Technical Skills:

- Programming
- Data Analysis
- Graphic Design

☐ Project Management
(The above are only examples; please customize to suit your needs)
Product Knowledge
☐ Product A
☐ Product B
☐ Product C

4. Training Preferences:
What format do you prefer for training? (Select all that apply)
☐ In-Person Workshops
☐ Virtual Training
☐ Self-Paced E-Learning
☐ Blended Learning (Combination of In-Person and Virtual)

5. Specific Training Needs:
What specific skills or knowledge areas do you feel you need improvement in?

6. Career Development:
Are there any skills or certifications you believe would contribute to your career development within the company?

Vendor Evaluation Scorecard

Selecting the right training vendor is critical for the success of your training programs. This vendor evaluation scorecard provides a structured approach to evaluating potential training vendors and ensuring alignment with your organization's requirements. You can use this as a template to assess potential training vendors:

Vendor Evaluation Scorecard

Vendor Name:
Date of Evaluation:
Evaluator:

Criteria:

Reputation and Track Record:
- ✓ Vendor's years of experience in the industry:
- ✓ Number of clients served:
- ✓ Client testimonials and references:

Customization Capabilities:
- ✓ Ability to tailor training programs to our organization's needs:
- ✓ Examples of customized training programs:

Cost vs. Quality:
- ✓ Cost of training services:
- ✓ Quality of training content and delivery:

Training Delivery Methods:
- ✓ Suitability of delivery methods (in-person, virtual, blended):
- ✓ Technology and resources for virtual training:

Compliance and Legal Considerations:
- ✓ Adherence to legal and ethical training practices:
- ✓ Data security measures in place:

Innovation and Technology:
- ✓ Integration of technology for interactive learning:
- ✓ Use of modern training platforms and tools:

Feedback and Continuous Improvement:
- ✓ Processes for collecting participant feedback:
- ✓ Strategies for continuous improvement:

Scoring:
- ✓ Each criterion will be scored on a scale of 1 to 5, with 5 being the highest score.
- ✓ Total Score (Sum of individual scores):

Overall Assessment:
- ✓ Based on the total score, provide an overall assessment of the vendor's suitability for our organization's training needs:

Training Program Evaluation Form

Evaluating training programs is essential to gauge their effectiveness. This sample training program evaluation format allows participants to provide valuable feedback, which can be used to refine future training initiatives.

Training Program Evaluation Form

Training Program Name: Date of Training: Trainer's Name:

Participant Information:

Name:

Department/Team:

Job Title:

Training Content Evaluation:

Please rate the following aspects of the training program on a scale of 1 to 5, with 5 being the highest score.

- ✓ Relevance of Content:
  The content was relevant to my job: [1] [2] [3] [4] [5]
- ✓ Clarity of Content:
  The content was presented clearly and understandably: [1] [2] [3] [4] [5]
- ✓ Engagement Level:
  The training materials and activities kept me engaged: [1] [2] [3] [4] [5]
- ✓ Interaction and Participation:
  Opportunities for interaction and participation were provided: [1] [2] [3] [4] [5]

Trainer Evaluation:

- ✓ Trainer Knowledge:
  The trainer demonstrated a strong knowledge of the subject matter: [1] [2] [3] [4] [5]
- ✓ Communication Skills:

The trainer effectively communicated ideas and concepts: [1] [2] [3] [4] [5]
- ✓ Facilitation Skills:
The trainer facilitated discussions and activities effectively: [1] [2] [3] [4] [5]

Overall Assessment:
- ✓ Please provide an overall assessment of the training program, considering its content and the trainer's performance:

Suggestions for Improvement:
- ✓ Are there any specific areas of the training program that you believe could be improved? Please provide suggestions:

Additional Comments:
- ✓ Any additional comments or feedback about the training program:

Legal and Ethical Training Resources

Legal and ethical considerations are essential in training. These resources serve as references for organizations looking to stay compliant with legal and ethical standards in their training initiatives. It is essential to customize this appendix with specific resources that pertain to your industry and region. Below, we list some resources that organizations can refer to for guidance:

- ✓ Legal and Compliance Training Resources:
[Insert relevant legal compliance websites or resources specific to your industry and region.]
- ✓ Diversity, Equity, and Inclusion (DEI) Training Resources:
[Insert relevant DEI training organizations or resources that promote diversity and inclusion.]

- ✓ Data Privacy and Security Resources:
  [Insert resources related to data privacy laws such as GDPR or HIPAA, and data security best practices.]
- ✓ Intellectual Property Protection Resources:
  [Insert resources related to copyright and intellectual property protection, including government agencies or legal organizations.]

Templates and Checklists for Training Initiatives

These templates and checklists provide a structured framework for planning, conducting, and evaluating training initiatives. Managers can customize them to suit their specific training needs and organizational requirements, ensuring the success of their training programs.

Training Project Plan Template:

A training project plan is essential for organizing and managing training initiatives effectively. It outlines the scope, objectives, tasks, timelines, and responsibilities. Here's a simplified template:

Training Project Plan

Project Title: [Training Program Name]

Project Overview:

- Project Objectives: [List the specific objectives of the training program.]
- Scope: [Define the scope of the training, including target audience, topics, and duration.]
- Key Stakeholders: [List key individuals or departments involved in the project.]

Project Timeline:

- Start Date: [Insert start date]
- End Date: [Insert end date]

Task List:

- Needs Assessment: Conduct a needs assessment to identify training gaps.
- Content Development: Create training materials and modules.
- Trainer Selection: Select and train trainers/facilitators.

- ☐ Schedule Training Sessions: Set training dates and times.
- ☐ Training Delivery: Conduct training sessions.
- ☐ Evaluation: Assess the effectiveness of the training.
- ☐ Feedback and Adjustments: Collect participant feedback and make necessary adjustments.

Responsibilities:
- ☐ Project Manager: [Name]
- ☐ Training Coordinator: [Name]
- ☐ Trainers: [List trainer names]

Resources Required:
- ☐ Training materials
- ☐ Training venue
- ☐ Audiovisual equipment

Budget:
- ☐ Total Budget: [Insert total budget]
- ☐ Actual Expenditure: [Track actual expenditure]

Training Needs Assessment Template:

A Training Needs Assessment helps identify the gaps in knowledge, skills, and behaviors that training programs should address. Here's a template:

Training Needs Assessment

Department/Team: [Insert Department/Team Name]
Assessment Date: [Insert Date]
Assessment Areas:
- ☐ Product Knowledge
- ☐ Technical Skills
- ☐ Soft Skills (e.g., Communication)
- ☐ Behavior and Attitude

Assessment Methods:
- ☐ Surveys
- ☐ Interviews
- ☐ Performance Data

- ☐ Observation

Assessment Findings:

Product Knowledge:
- ☐ Gap Identified: [Describe the knowledge gap.]
- ☐ Recommended Training: [Suggest relevant training programs.]

Technical Skills:

- ☐ Gap Identified: [Describe the skill gap.]
- ☐ Recommended Training: [Suggest relevant training programs.]

Soft Skills:
- ☐ Gap Identified: [Describe the soft skill gap.]
- ☐ Recommended Training: [Suggest relevant soft skills training.]

Behavior and Attitude:
- ☐ Gap Identified: [Describe the behavioral or attitude gap.]
- ☐ Recommended Training: [Suggest relevant training programs.]

Training Priority:
- ☐ High Priority: [List areas that require immediate attention.]
- ☐ Medium Priority: [List areas that should be addressed soon.]
- ☐ Low Priority: [List areas that can be addressed later.]

Training Evaluation Checklist:

Evaluating training programs is crucial to measure their effectiveness. Here's a checklist for evaluating a training program:

Training Evaluation Checklist

Training Program Name: [Insert Program Name]

Evaluation Date: [Insert Date]

Participant Information:
- [ ] Attendance Record
- [ ] Pre-training Knowledge Assessment

Training Content Evaluation:
- [ ] Relevance of Content
- [ ] Clarity of Content
- [ ] Engagement Level
- [ ] Interaction and Participation

Trainer Evaluation:
- [ ] Trainer Knowledge
- [ ] Communication Skills
- [ ] Facilitation Skills

Learning Outcomes:
- [ ] Post-training Knowledge Assessment
- [ ] Skill Demonstration (if applicable)

Feedback and Improvement:
- [ ] Participant Feedback
- [ ] Trainer Feedback
- [ ] Observations and Notes
- [ ] Suggestions for Improvement

Overall Assessment:
- [ ] Training Program Effectiveness
- [ ] Areas Needing Improvement

Follow-Up Actions:
- [ ] Adjustments to Training Content
- [ ] Additional Training Sessions (if necessary)
- [ ] Feedback Incorporation into Future Programs

Sample Training Program Outlines

These sample training program outlines provide a structured framework for designing and conducting effective training programs in leadership development, on-boarding, technical skills, and soft skills training. Managers can adapt and customize these outlines to meet their specific training needs and objectives.

1. Leadership Development Program Outline:

Program Title: Leadership Excellence Program
Program Overview:
Program Duration: 6 months
Target Audience: Mid-level managers and emerging leaders
Program Objectives:
- ✓ Develop leadership skills and competencies.
- ✓ Foster a culture of innovation and collaboration.
- ✓ Prepare participants for higher leadership roles.

Program Components:
Module 1: Leadership Fundamentals (Month 1)
- ✓ Leadership theories and models
- ✓ Effective communication and active listening
- ✓ Conflict resolution and decision-making

Module 2: Leading Teams (Month 2-3)
- ✓ Team dynamics and building high-performing teams
- ✓ Emotional intelligence and leadership styles
- ✓ Motivation and employee engagement

Module 3: Strategic Leadership (Month 4-5)

- ✓ Strategic planning and goal setting
- ✓ Change management and adaptability

Leading in a VUCA (volatile, uncertain, complex, ambiguous) world

Module 4: Leadership Capstone Project (Month 6)
- ✓ Participants apply learned skills to a real-world project.
- ✓ Presentation of project outcomes and leadership growth.

Assessment and Evaluation:
- ✓ Monthly assessments, self-reflection, and peer evaluations.
- ✓ Leadership competency assessments.
- ✓ Capstone project evaluation.

2. On-boarding Program Outline:

Program Title: New Employee On-boarding Program
Program Overview:
Program Duration: 1 week
Target Audience: New hires across all departments
Program Objectives:
- ✓ Ensure a smooth transition for new employees.
- ✓ Introduce company culture, policies, and expectations.
- ✓ Equip new hires with essential job-related knowledge and skills.

Program Components:
Day 1: Welcome and Orientation
- ✓ Welcome session with senior leadership.
- ✓ Company history, mission, and values.
- ✓ HR and administrative on-boarding.

Day 2-3: Departmental On-boarding
- ✓ Department-specific training and introductions.
- ✓ Job-specific training and role expectations.

✓ Team introductions and ice-breaking activities.

Day 4: Compliance and Policies
- ✓ HR policies, benefits, and procedures.
- ✓ Safety and security protocols.
- ✓ Ethical guidelines and code of conduct.

Day 5: Tools and Resources
- ✓ IT and technology orientation.
- ✓ Access to tools, systems, and resources.
- ✓ Final Q&A and feedback session.

Assessment and Evaluation:
- ✓ Feedback surveys from new employees.
- ✓ Assessment of job-specific competencies.
- ✓ Continuous feedback and mentorship during the probationary period.

3. Technical Skills Training Program Outline:

Program Title: Advanced Data Analytics Training

Program Overview:

Program Duration: 8 weeks

Target Audience: Data analysts and data scientists

Program Objectives:
- ✓ Enhance technical skills in data analysis and modeling.
- ✓ Apply advanced analytics techniques to real-world data sets.
- ✓ Prepare participants for complex data-driven projects.

Program Components:

Weeks 1-2: Data Fundamentals
- ✓ Data types, structures, and storage.
- ✓ Data cleaning and preprocessing.
- ✓ Introduction to data visualization tools.

Weeks 3-4: Statistical Analysis
- ✓ Descriptive and inferential statistics.

- ✓ Hypothesis testing and confidence intervals.
- ✓ Regression analysis.

Weeks 5-6: Machine Learning
- ✓ Machine learning algorithms (e.g., decision trees, SVM).
- ✓ Model evaluation and hyper-parameter tuning.
- ✓ Supervised and unsupervised learning.

Weeks 7-8: Real-World Projects
- ✓ Participants work on real data analytics projects.
- ✓ Presentation of project findings and recommendations.

Assessment and Evaluation:
- ✓ Continuous assessments, quizzes, and hands-on exercises.
- ✓ Evaluation of project outcomes and presentations.
- ✓ Skills assessment and certification.

4. Soft Skills Training Program Outline:

Program Title: Effective Communication and Interpersonal Skills

Program Overview:

Program Duration: 4 weeks

Target Audience: All employees, especially those in client-facing roles

Program Objectives:
- ✓ Improve communication skills.
- ✓ Enhance interpersonal effectiveness.
- ✓ Foster positive workplace relationships.

Program Components:

Week 1: Communication Foundations
- ✓ Verbal and non-verbal communication.
- ✓ Active listening and empathy.
- ✓ Communicating with clarity and confidence.

Week 2: Interpersonal Skills
- ✓ Building rapport and trust.
- ✓ Conflict resolution and negotiation.
- ✓ Cross-cultural communication.

Week 3: Presentation Skills
- ✓ Effective public speaking.
- ✓ Creating impactful presentations.
- ✓ Handling questions and feedback.

Week 4: Practical Application
- ✓ Role-play scenarios and case studies.
- ✓ Peer feedback and improvement.
- ✓ Graduation ceremony and certificates.

Assessment and Evaluation:
- ✓ Skill demonstrations through role-plays.
- ✓ Peer and trainer evaluations.
- ✓ Self-assessment and reflection exercises.

The Future of Employee Training

As we come to the conclusion of this comprehensive guide on employee training, it is essential to reflect on the key concepts and insights we've explored throughout this journey. In this concluding chapter, we will recap the fundamental principles, delve into the pivotal role of HR and corporate leadership, and emphasize the ongoing nature of employee training in shaping the future of organizations.

Recap of Key Concepts

Throughout this book, we've delved into a myriad of concepts, strategies, and best practices in employee training. These key takeaways include:

- ✓ **Importance of Training:** Training is not just a cost but an investment in human capital, leading to improved performance, job satisfaction, and organizational success.
- ✓ **Measuring ROI:** Evaluating the return on investment (ROI) of training programs is crucial to assess their effectiveness and make data-driven decisions.
- ✓ **Assessing Training Needs:** Identifying and addressing specific training needs, including product knowledge, skills, behavior, and attitude, is the foundation of successful training initiatives.
- ✓ **Selecting the Right Vendor:** Careful consideration in choosing training vendors can significantly impact program quality and success.
- ✓ **Planning and Implementation:** Developing a comprehensive training strategy, designing effective modules, and choosing the right

delivery methods are essential steps in the training process.

- ✓ **Emerging Trends:** Staying updated with technology-driven training solutions, microlearning, gamification, and adaptive learning is critical for future-proofing training programs.
- ✓ **Fostering a Learning Culture:** Encouraging continuous learning, career development, feedback, and self-directed learning creates a culture of growth and innovation.
- ✓ **Measuring Impact:** The impact of training should be measured through Kirkpatrick's Four Levels of Evaluation, relevant metrics, data-driven decision-making, and continuous improvement strategies.
- ✓ **Legal and Ethical Considerations:** Compliance training, diversity and inclusion training, data security, and intellectual property protection are essential aspects of ethical and legal training.
- ✓ **Case Studies:** Real-world examples illustrate how organizations have successfully implemented training programs to achieve their goals.

The Role of HR and Corporate Leadership

Human Resources (HR) and corporate leadership play pivotal roles in the success of training programs. HR serves as the architect of training initiatives, from identifying needs to designing content and measuring outcomes. Corporate leadership, including executives and managers, must champion training and actively participate in it. Their commitment sets the tone for the entire organization and reinforces the importance of ongoing learning and development.

HR's role includes:

Conducting thorough needs assessments to pinpoint training requirements.

- ✓ Developing comprehensive training strategies that align with organizational goals.
- ✓ Collaborating with training vendors or in-house teams to create effective content.
- ✓ Ensuring the efficient delivery of training through various methods.
- ✓ Monitoring and evaluating training programs to make necessary adjustments.
- ✓ Championing a culture of continuous learning and career development.

Corporate leadership's role includes:

- ✓ Demonstrating a commitment to training by actively participating in programs.
- ✓ Communicating the strategic importance of training to the entire organization.
- ✓ Setting an example by engaging in continuous learning and personal development.
- ✓ Supporting employees' training efforts through mentorship and resources.
- ✓ Encouraging a culture of feedback, innovation, and knowledge sharing.

The Ongoing Journey of Employee Training

Employee training is not a destination but an ongoing journey. As the business landscape evolves, organizations must adapt to remain competitive. This requires a commitment to continuous learning and development at all levels. The future of employee training will be shaped by emerging technologies, changing workforce dynamics, and evolving skill requirements.

To ensure the ongoing success of employee training:
- ✓ Embrace technology-driven solutions, such as AI-powered learning platforms and virtual reality simulations.
- ✓ Emphasize microlearning and on-demand training to meet the needs of a mobile and fast-paced workforce.
- ✓ Utilize gamification and employee engagement strategies to enhance training effectiveness.
- ✓ Personalize learning experiences through adaptive learning algorithms.
- ✓ Foster a culture of continuous learning, where employees are encouraged to take ownership of their development.
- ✓ Promote career development and growth opportunities to retain top talent.
- ✓ Leverage data and analytics for data-driven decision-making and continuous improvement.
- ✓ Stay attuned to legal and ethical considerations in training, adapting to evolving regulations.

In conclusion, employee training is a dynamic and transformative force within organizations. It empowers individuals to grow, adapt, and excel in their roles, ultimately driving organizational success. By embracing the principles and strategies outlined in this book and committing to the ongoing journey of employee training, organizations can position themselves to thrive in an ever-changing business landscape, fostering innovation, employee satisfaction, and long-term growth.

Conclusion

As we reach the culmination of our journey through the world of employee training, we pause to reflect on the valuable insights and strategies that have unfolded before us. '**The Ultimate Employee Training Guide:** *Training Today, Leading Tomorrow*' has served as your guide, offering a comprehensive exploration of the intricate art of training and development.

In these pages, we've delved into the evolution of employee training, tracing its roots from conventional classroom settings to the dynamic and tech-driven landscape of today. We've unearthed the undeniable benefits of training, from enhanced productivity to improved job satisfaction, and we've explored the sobering repercussions that organizations face when they neglect this essential investment.

We've dissected training as an investment, examining the intricacies of Return on Investment (ROI). Real-life case studies have illustrated how training, when executed effectively, can generate tangible returns, not only in financial terms but also in the enrichment of an organization's human capital.

Understanding the various facets of training needs assessment has equipped you to identify product knowledge gaps, perform skills assessments, evaluate behavior and attitude, and select the most suitable tools and methods to assess these critical areas.

Choosing the right training vendor is an art in itself. We've provided you with the criteria, insights, and considerations necessary to make informed decisions, ensuring your training initiatives align perfectly with your organization's goals and values.

In the heart of training, we've explored the meticulous planning and implementation of training programs. You've learned to craft a robust training strategy, design modules that resonate with learners, and adapt your delivery methods to suit the ever-evolving preferences of your audience. Monitoring and evaluation have emerged as your allies in this endeavor, offering continuous refinement and improvement of your training programs.

Peering into the future, we've glimpsed the technological advancements and trends that are shaping the landscape of employee training. Technology-driven solutions, microlearning, gamification, and personalization are set to transform the way we educate and upskill our workforce.

But training extends far beyond the confines of a single program or session. We've explored the creation of a culture of continuous learning within your organization, fostering career development, seeking employee feedback, and encouraging self-directed learning.

The meticulous measurement of training's impact has been a recurring theme throughout our journey. You've gained insights into Kirkpatrick's Four Levels of Evaluation, discovered the metrics for success, embraced data-driven decision-making, and committed to the pursuit of continuous improvement.

Ethical and legal considerations have underpinned our exploration, ensuring that your training programs are not only effective but also compliant, inclusive, and respectful of intellectual property.

Our path culminates in the illumination of successful case studies from diverse industries, serving as beacons of inspiration for your own training initiatives.

As we close this chapter of our journey, it is essential to acknowledge the central role that HR and corporate leadership play in the success of training programs. Your dedication to nurturing and empowering your workforce is the cornerstone of organizational growth and resilience.

The journey does not conclude here; it merely evolves. The future of employee training holds exciting possibilities, innovations, and opportunities. As the world continues to change, adapt, and advance, so too will the realm of training and development.

We extend our heartfelt gratitude for joining us on this transformative voyage through the world of training. As you venture forth, armed with knowledge, strategies, and a deep commitment to your workforce, remember that the power to empower lies within you.

May your dedication to training transformation continue to shape a future where organizations thrive, individuals flourish, and possibilities remain boundless.

About the Author
'GERARD ASSEY'

Gerard Assey is a Graduate in Economics, a PGD in Management (HRD) and holds a Doctorate in Leadership. Gerard holds several International Qualifications in Sales, Debt Collection, Training & Teaching, and is a 'Fellow' of the prestigious 'Institute of Sales & Marketing Management'-UK, a Certified NLP Practitioner, a 'Certified Trainer', an 'Accredited Management Teacher-Behavioral Sciences', a 'Certified Competency Facilitator', a 'Certified Management Consultant'- (the International credentials of a professional management consultant, awarded in accordance with global standards of the ICMCI); and a Certification from the University of Michigan in 'Successful Negotiation: Essential Strategies and Skills'
He is also a Member of the 'National Association of Sales Professionals' backed with several years experience in varied industries, both in India and Overseas. He also holds an 'Etiquette Consultant' Certification from the USA (by Sue Fox, Author of Best Seller: 'Business Etiquette for Dummies'. She has trained some of the top celebrities' world over). He was also a recipient of a scholarship for extensive training in Japan on 'Corporate Management for India'.
Gerard Assey is 'Founder & Chief Corporate Trainer' of the Group: '**Citius, Altius, Fortius Unlimited**'- an organization that **celebrated 20 years of Glorious Service** in 2021, focusing on 3 Core Competencies:

People. Performance. Profit; in functional areas of Sales & Marketing, HR & Organizational Development, covering Recruitment, Training & Consultancy!

Having managed organizations with large Sales Forces in India & Overseas, his specialization cover extensive areas of Sales Training (All levels - Presentation, Negotiation, Key/ Strategic Accounts Management & Managerial Skills for all sectors), Bid Proposal/ Capture Planning/ Management Trainings, Retail Sales, Customer Service & Customer Retention Programs, Training for Prevention & Collection of Debt, Self & Personal Development Programs (Time Management, Teamwork & Team Building, Business Etiquette & Personal Grooming, Leadership & Managerial Skills, People Management Skills, Train-the-Trainer etc), including preparation of Custom-designed Business Manuals for Internal (HR, Induction, and Sales etc) & External use (Instruction, User Manuals).

Gerard has successfully conducted over 6060 Trainings & Workshops (as of Feb '24) all across India, Middle East, Africa, Europe & S.E. Asia. Besides public programs conducted regularly, both in India & Overseas, he has some of the top names as clients whom he services from Single Owners to large Public & Government undertakings, covering all sectors, for their in-house needs.

His website: www.CollectionSkills.com is the only one in this part of the world to be featured in the 'Collections & Credit Risk Magazine-USA' under 'Who's Who in Training' and ranks TOP, along with other websites listed below on most search engines.

Gerard is author of 109 books already (Feb 2024)

A few of our business related books:

1. Bite-sized Bits on Commonsense Management
2. Heart to Heart on Life's Principles'
3. How to become a Successful Manager
4. The Sales Professionals' Master Workbook of S.Y.S.T.E.M.S
5. The Professional Business Email Etiquette Handbook & Guide
6. The Professional Business Video-Conferencing Etiquette Handbook & Guide
7. Professional Presentation Skills
8. Exceptional Customer Service
9. Professional Tele-Marketing Skills
10. Professional Debt Collection Skills
11. The G.R.E.A.T. Sales & Service Workbook
12. Sales Training Advantage for Results (*The Ultimate Sales Training Manual to enable you stand out as a S.T.A.R.*)
13. CEO Daily Planner & Organizer
14. The Sales Professionals' Master Daily Planner
15. The Professional Debt Collector's Master Daily Planner
16. My Daily Planner & Organizer
17. MY EMERGENCY INFORMATION RECORD (Family Emergency & Peace of Mind Planner)
18. The Ultimate Therapist & Counselors Planner and Organizer
19. Building an Ethical Workplace
20. Managing Relationships at Work
21. Managing Business Meetings Effectively
22. Effective Delegation Skills
23. Goal Setting for Success
24. B2B Selling by Email
25. Professional Business Etiquette & Grooming
26. Dining Etiquette & Table Manners
27. Effective Networking Skills
28. Grooming, Etiquette & Manners for Teens, Young Adults & Future Leaders
29. Inter-Personal Skills
30. Get Ready, Get Hired!
31. Selling in a Recession
32. Effective Receivables Management in an Economic Downturn!
33. Real Estate & Property Sales Training

Besides regularly contributing to business & trade journals, including international ones such as the 'Creative Training Techniques' and the 'Sales News' of the U.S.A, He is also a member of several prestigious bodies & trade associations, having participated in many Conferences & Workshops in India & Overseas.

Prior to his last assignment of leading & managing a large MNC as head, Gerard had a 3-year stint in the Middle East as a Consultant with a leading British Consultancy Firm.

As the past 'Official Country Representative' for the International Business Award- 'THE STEVIES'-(the business world's own Oscar) for about 4 years- he ensured a few Indian companies that qualify for the same every year!

Gerard can be contacted at:
Email: <u>training@Sales-Training.in</u>,<u>training@CollectionSkills.com</u>
Websites:

        <u>www.Sales-Training.in</u>
        <u>www.EtiquetteWorks.in</u>
        <u>www.CollectionSkills.com</u>
        <u>www.RetailSalesTraining.in</u>
        <u>www.SalesTrainingIndia.com</u>
        <u>www.ManualPreparation.com</u>
        <u>www.TrainingWithPuppets.com</u>
        <u>www.FirstContactAcademy.com</u>
        <u>www.SalesAndMarketingRecruiter.com</u>

Our TRAININGS that can help your team

- ✓ **Sales Effectiveness**: Selling Skills for any Sector: Service/ Logistics/ FMCG Realty/ Insurance & Finance/ Media/ SPA's, Health Clubs & Salons/ Key Account Management, Effective Negotiation Skills/ Bid & Proposal Management Skills/ Retail Sales Training: Any Sector (Auto, Jewelry, Clothing, Luxury etc)
- ✓ **Customer Service Skills**-Complaints Handling & Customer Retention
- ✓ **Debt Prevention & Collection Skills**
- ✓ **Etiquette & Grooming**
- ✓ **Leadership & Managerial Skills**
- ✓ **Self & Personal Development Skills**: Presentation Skills/ Effective Communication Skills/Business Proposal Writing Skills/ Problem Solving & Decision Making Skills/ Empowering Secretaries-The perfect PA! (For Secretaries & PA's)/ Effective Time Management/ Teamwork & Teambuilding/ P.R.I.D.E- **P**ersonal **R**esponsibility **I**n **D**elivering **E**xcellence